YOU DO NOT HAVE TO BE GOOD

You Do Not Have To Be Good

poems by Madeleine Barnes

Barnes, Madeleine
1st edition

ISBN: 978-1-949487-04-6
Library of Congress Control Number: 2020935052

Interior layout by Matt Mauch
Cover design by Joel Coggins
Editing by Matt Mauch and Sara Lefsyk

Trio House Press, Inc.
Ponte Vedra Beach, FL

To contact the author, send an email to tayveneese@gmail.com.

*For my family, and for all queer disabled women
and non-binary folks everywhere*

TABLE OF CONTENTS

VALOR / 87

YOU DO NOT HAVE TO KNOW

YOU DO NOT HAVE TO CREATE PARADISE

YOU DO NOT HAVE TO MEASURE
THE LONGITUDE AND LATITUDE

YOU DO NOT HAVE TO BE RIGOROUS

YOU DO NOT HAVE TO PROVE IT

. . . there
were no stars, just the weather of childhood
where it's snowing forever.

– Carl Phillips

YOU DO NOT HAVE TO BE EARTHLY

FORTY BLACK SHIPS

I was dressing her in armor for the war.
I guided her feet into bronze socks,

helped her step into netted yellow pants,
tied her shins with quilted grids of gold.

Crinet, grangaurd, shoulder plates.
It was almost time, but I didn't know.

And when the nurse knocked I helped her
rise from the violet bed. And when I

dispatched her into the battlefield, I said:
take my spears and black-tipped arrows.

Run toward your mother, and her mother.
I will follow soon when I find the right plates

to cover my trembling breastbone.
I'll come when I cannot see you anymore

but for now, my shield, my daggers,
forty black ships in the sea offshore.

I was sure that she could not hear me weeping
as I lowered the helmet over her curls
and kissed the heavy visor.

SURROUND HER WITH COLORS

Step one: Andromeda. Step two: dark eyelashes.

Step three: adulthood with faint traces of childhood.

Stabilizer: On. Auto-focus: off. Love

how she touches you. Think: the stars are planning

the erasure of two-hundred-year-old silences,

so let her try to reach you. Step five: look at her

without expressing fear. Draw a tarot card

and let her tell you what it means.

Give her a crown of almonds and wet grass.

Frame something teal, something velvet,

something worthy. Give her a cathedral,

an amber glove, remix raspberry and neon.

Give her a lilac cube, enamored hi-shine,

avalanche of electric violet.

Cover her in changeable taffeta and ginger root.

Love her vices, her moss and copper.

Bring your relics. Step seven: sing.

A FIRE

At her funeral I wondered
if I wasn't really dead, too.

Fine gold—the gold of her hair
rubbed by rain, gold behind my eyes

flint-like, petrified everything.
All I could do was tend to it,

usher in bronze and phosphorescence,
build my grief a fine and flaming crown.

Snow filled the corridor
where we prayed her luminous

and gestured toward heaven,
blessed her, but she didn't answer.

Afterwards, I tended bar,
poured wine and whiskey

to distract the living
from their half-belief.

When the blaze closed in,
I did not want to talk

about things to come
or comfort others.

I kept my anguish close,
set foot in the fire as if

I could simply remind "her,"
a her "undone," that I was

molten at my very core—
and she'd appear by my side.

Dana: sense of reflection.

Jayda: strong feelings of someone unknown; personal. Setting at bar is confusing to connect the two poems.

16

PERENNIALS

When they gave her CPR, it was because her body
was not *her* anymore. I said nothing because

there was blood running from a cut beneath
her hairline. I said nothing because everything

fell apart in my mouth into piles of razors
that severed language, my only tether to earth,

to her, and cut a hole in the crowd that surrounded
the open ambulance as it flashed its crown

into the corners of Union Square. Four policemen
ran up the subway stairs, puffed the fall air

that once belonged to her. I wish I had wrapped her
in blankets, bandages, numbed out the sting

of how easily we are forgotten. I wish
I could leave irises on the porch of the woman

who walked into the shop at midnight,
that the sirens were remnants of churchbells,

cymbals, secondhand static. There were needles
and black thread, white gloves, sheets, a stretcher.

I wish I had asked her: *how can I help you?* But she fell—
I was frightened by the pitch of my own breathing.

Lassiter:
Confusing
paralysis.

Alex:
confusion of
the afterlife.

El J:
Isolation of
parts.
contained
grief.
silenced
bar was like
a comfort
setting.

1) p. 16-17

- Noticed Barnes talked about a woman's body almost burned from "A Fire".

- Noticed in "Perennials" that "her body was not "her" anymore." Some type of resurrection story or spiritual type of union.

- Question: Between the two poems can you see a certain narrative that connects to the thoughts I said?

FORMS OF SUSPENSION

I see the bird drop from the edge of the window
and smash itself under tire after tire.

It matters as much as a footstep, particles drifting too slowly
to ever really die—one body of air lifting off of a surface

and landing over itself. I am looking for safety in a crushed bird,
want its power and dumb luck to generate new softness.

Its body piles light into the cement, reflection flickering off a passing car's
metal door. Something better is waiting, it confirms, it goes on forever
between two places, chooses, and makes a transition.

SLEEP PHASE

The forest again, this time in winter, and with us,
disembodied voices: the bend in the tree,
the blank stretch of highway glimmering.
At the park entrance, a bucket of antlers waits
to be gathered up. It's normal to start out here,
standing before the aisle of firs where dark eyes
hang. The forest can only be motionless now,
and there is no because. Brown needles underfoot.
I thought that if we drank enough we wouldn't
wind up here, where the path begins, light gone,
the river locked shut. I've done something wrong.
There's a wound in my sleep and I cannot see it,
a diamond, a tradition lost, in a cabin far ahead.
I'm tired of cold animals regarding me as something
intergalactic, hard to please. I see my own soul's
femaleness. I'm afraid it isn't safe. I look at you,
silvery and scratched, marked by a different suffering,
the kind that stays away from new fires. Have I done
something wrong? And now, the world cleared away,
a flame expanding, tell me, will I be able
to speak in the end? Tell me. Stay calm.

YOU DO NOT HAVE TO SEDUCE

VULNERARY

He brought me to a field
and led me to the cabin
where he was living like Thoreau.

Tufts of green laced the mud.
I stood and marveled
at the bare room

while egrets landed
like slender teeth
in the marsh,

their wingbeats
tapping out
a song: not-now.

Finely divided leaves
of yarrow surrounded
the porch. The plant's

chief use
is to stop
the bleeding of wounds.

He was my teacher.
He wanted me
to kiss him.

I told him
what I knew
of nature:

Valerian has white
to pale lavender
flowers,

Angelica, dark
purple stems, weak leaves,
stronger roots and seeds,

that even botanists have died
from mistaking Water Hemlock
for Angelica.

Who knows why
I choked down
my dream of poison.

What will heal me
still sleeps somewhere
in those woods.

INCIDENT ON THE TRAM

The girl on the tram without a ticket
is forced off the car between stations.
The officer has different colored eyebrows.
He speaks harshly and spits at her shoes.

Seven hundred crowns, he says to her in English.
She shows him her wallet, five American dollars,
a medical card. A large yellow leaf is stuck
below her heel. When he twists her arm,

her shoes make no utterance. Two hundred
hours from now, four thousand miles overseas,
her mother will drop the phone. In three hundred hours,
the news will air. They will have found her clothes.

The tram doors open and he pulls her off.
The passengers stare in different directions
while the fields change color, full of testimonies.
Something about the way he struck her head

to wake her—*did he have a badge?* A pin drops.
The tram makes its way through the mountains.
She is walking at night on the path
beside the river. Cables shudder overhead,

making their secret violent connections,
her voice a wire so thin
it cannot be traced to a body.

I WILL TELL YOU EVERYTHING

Today a stranger grabbed me by the arm,
pulled an exaggerated bruise from my skin,

a hyacinth in her brown shopping bag
passing on its memory of living
inside tenderness for hurried people.

Maybe she thought I was floating away,
maybe she thought I could be her sister.

You touch the pearls of my spine that emerge
when I bend to slip off my pointed shoe,
you must see how my body shakes and swells,

you must be the strong place I return to
because you say you saw something lovely

on your way home from work, hundreds
of bats blooming from treetops along the highway
in a crazed swarm, diving in all directions.

What-now my heartbeat whispers to itself,
fluttering above things too small to see.

YOU DO NOT HAVE TO EXPLAIN
TENDERNESS

NIGHT WORK

My father held a tiny piece of glass
that glittered in his hand
as we walked out into night
into the company of hills
and shambling sheep,
boots pressed against thistledown
and when we were two hours away
from the eclipse, he held the lens
in front of my eyes and I saw
another thing, the bigger thing.
I was afraid and shut my eyes.
The muscles around my heart
tightened as we walked
toward the end of comprehension
exchanging light waves
in silence. It will happen again
in twenty years, he said.
Cautious, coordinating,
Things you know by sight.
Things you know without.

TENDERNESS IS ALL I REMEMBER

You are far off but I am right here writing,
glinting, nearing you, just southwest of you,

a sea away, waiting to kiss a star against your
cheekbone, because separation presses hard

armor into my gray, angled apartment.
Sister, what do you think will happen to us?

Do you think it is plausible that we,
winged, will trim the ghosts' gowns

from snow? Do you wonder how
ownership renders need and dangerous

surroundings, our world drowned,
and then adorned? I want to be your one

stone, nest, entrance. From here:
treetops, nightclubs, units of tin.

In this moment of missing you
I am within hundreds of minutes

of seeing you, knowing you, born, reborn,
grown, with hits of thin nights vivid

as this one, almost closer, the two of us found
underneath the edifice of each other's homes.

TO CHARGE FORWARD

We climb steps toward a beach without fences,
our veins full of glitter and the metallic gifts of childhood

as if we might forget ourselves before the sea, offset
the light of speculation from which we always retreated

simply by looking upwards, or by giving our hearts
to one thing and not the rest. We admire

the birds of winter, how they seem unaware
of their authority, self-mastered, floating on a black wave.

We can no longer say, "that's you," or "that's me."
The wind pleads like a saw against our throats,

our lungs, our terror. We stand in the clear and quiet
landscape, overtaken—the wind presses against us harder.

Side by side, we understand nothing, dependent
on mysterious images that enter us.

Perseus, the constellation of our mother and father,
infuses us with calm expectancy.

They, too, freed themselves of dread.
They, too, ran into the open.

THE MARK MY BODY DRAWS IN LIGHT

These books have my mother's hands
and when I hold them I believe I have become her.

This is my chest that rises, I say. *These are my knuckles.*
From my mother I learned to speak slowly, to wrap

my words like scarves around the necks of strangers.
I learned my bones are framework for loss, for pages

stripped free of information. The books are restless
and open in their sleep. *Read this,* she would say

with a fistful of chimney smoke. *You'll like this one,*
breath white as wildfire. I learned from my mother

to consider my shadow, the dark cast off by shins,
the calves, by hair shaken out from the root, the mark

my body draws in light. I learned to read the shore
with my vertebrae, arms outstretched to a pitchfork sky.

I hemmed her skirt to the sand to anchor her, lace furled
in both hands. Once in our house she positioned a

flashlight, leapt into the otherwise pitch-dark living room,
lifted my hands to cast their weight into space.

The light that outlined us was piercing gold.

YOU DO NOT HAVE TO BE FRUITFUL

DIG

The two of us sit on the shore
throwing clementine peels into the sea.
Our bodies burn. We scoop the sand.

I pick up a hard shell lined with mother-of-pearl.
Oysters feed on the seabed, grow on stones.
They are at home on the posts of piers,

on the bark and stilt of mangrove trees.
Their fragility is a survival strategy.
I want her to gather the material she needs

to write her book. I drill ink into my brain.
She says, you taught me how to be a mother.
Too many stars span before us. We tear the rocks.

I dream of knowing my place in her poems
but bury my heart deep in the earth,
tiny gravedigger. I want to be joined

to her words, but how many times are you allowed
to need your mother? *Help me with this,*
I want to beg her. *Help me exit your poem.*

THE BLUE OF IT

Write the destination on your palm and buy
the ticket west. Your bed is a meteor flashing

at the center of your dream that you would do this
on the longest night of the year like a wolf

moving through the blue light in the fence.
Come on, pull on your black traveling boots.

This is a play about a painting of an ocean
and you are acting out the death of winter.

This is a painting about winter acting terribly
in a theater packed with snow. Come on,

the body is made through a series of skylights
where the sun is coming down. Peel a name

from the roof of your mouth and throw it against
the blinding white screen. Then look

into the silence until it begins an apology
full of sound. Move your eyes

to the train where they're now boarding.
Step away, you're in danger of being

erased by your own reflection: you
are dressed like a person who is ready

to outstrip, outshine, escape. You shouldn't
have to explain yourself to anyone, and yet

you're pleading with the sun to delay
the agony of loving every living thing.

YOU DO NOT HAVE TO BE CAPTIVE

SMALLNESS

If I love the spoon, the spoon
holds a concave hunger wreathed
in sugar. If I am sick, it is because
my cells are pinned to a belief
that sickness is desirable.
Or is it the funeral of words
swirling around the synagogue
in Cortona where everything
trembles after midnight?
It sings at a maddening pitch
that doubles itself in stillness.
There is a magnet inside the earth
that makes the ground jump.
The earth becomes the magnet.
If I desire smallness I focus on
the footsteps downstairs,
someone coming to see me,
climbing the sky and echoing
through clear space. They come
because they are ready to exist.
Their footsteps tell me nothing
about who they are.
If I desire smallness I walk
around the border of the city
deep in the flux of aimlessness.
How quickly the city
becomes a book of meetings.
If I desire smallness I walk
into a house where people
talk loudly to themselves
and escape from being seen.
They exist because they
are all that remains of me.

YOU DO NOT HAVE TO TAKE
MY WORD FOR IT

A DREAM IN MOTION

At first
you weren't old enough.
Then, you were.
In place
of your usual staccato,
there was silence.
In place
of your loneliness,
a camera. You think
these images
weren't meant
to imprison you.
Their iron bars
fall down when
the nightmares come.
At the bottom
of a swimming pool
you tell your enemy
you love her.
At the bottom
of the ski lift
you lose your shoe,
drop your phone
into the lake.
The gun fires
twice as you
pull out
your own rib.
You run
through your
high school
naked, in search
of the chemistry
lab. Tap
on his shoulder
but he won't
turn around.
There are lilacs
growing

underwater
but you are going
blind.

2) p. 42-43

- Noticed some of the lines of this "dream" sets somewhere in jail.

- Noticed raw emotion and some hallucination in attitude.

- Question: What the poet mean by "There are lilacs growing underwater but you are going blind?" Is it a nightmare, expression, what effects are taking place?

POEM COMPOSED IN THE ALPHABET BLADES

There is a shimmering excitement
in the language of scissors,
anonymous music
flung out of metallic light,
a sound like a cathedral's
stained glass softening the corner
of a hymnal, a rising cadence
in the secret way we talk.
I try to judge the hairline's evenness,
pulling your head gently to the left or right
considering your radiant ear.
I want to know what your mother knows:
the hidden purpose of your creation.
I want to know what your lover knows,
the secret inside your secrets,
the origin of the plot of thorns
that turns to knots in my comb.
I make promises to you while reaching
into the atmosphere of your trust.
It carries neither sun nor wind
only the honor of having,
in some way, shaped you.

FOLLOWING MY PARENTS WITH A CAMERA

As we cross the street I photograph their backs,
their silver dandelion hair and thin beach clothes,

the frail trampled brush and wild sea oats
that move in feathered arcs with the wind.

Out in the open my mother says she's sure
my partner's immigration papers will arrive soon,

and, however difficult it is to imagine,
we will find our way through this time,

this unfinished bloody star map of waiting.
Her words are a ship's light, a horoscope.

My father moves silently ahead and I watch
as I have always watched, record as I have always recorded.

It feels right, the three of us together, their slow attention,
the grit of their concern; there is no obstacle,

my sisters are asleep at the house as we adopt
our original, perfect configuration. *Do not enter.*

They had so many rules that I did not adhere to.
I went between them with devilish exuberance,

carved a place for myself where I was no longer cold.
Waves blur, the lens fogs, there is so much space for us.

The air bears down: the first time they brought me
to the ocean, the water rushed for my neck

and my father snatched me up like I was necessary.
This time I kneel before them as though we bear no relation

as they wave with their backs to the sea, the surf warmer
and more irreplaceably charged than I remember.

My adult self presses down, captures a bit of blood,
a half moon. I don't know how I came to know this:

the good in them is the good in me. It cannot be made
or unmade; it covers their whole bodies,

soars between them, edgeless. It was there before I sent for them,
I was a comet above a deserted beach shining and fierce,

not an archangel but an omen, a disturbance
that pulled between us like a leash, a cool, blue strand,

an attachment, and now it strains, tugs, proves
we have always been nowhere.

3) p. 45-46

- Noticed the photos that are being taken are mostly the parent's backs. Hardly a face showing
- Noticed tension on p. 46 from the first three lines like there's a murder.
- Noticed maybe the poet witnessed his parents disappearance of some sort.

- Question: unsure

WHAT HAPPENED

It's what she won't tell you.
A man you've never met.

It's *something must have happened here*
and something did.

It's having no idea what to do.
It's a pill that makes her quiet

instead of angry.
It's a man telling a girl

to use the word "I" less.
It's nights spent dancing

and nights spent walking in the snow
trying to start over.

It's the way she has to force herself
to leave the house,

a wind that lifts
and separates her hair.

It's the doctors who side
with her parents

and the teachers who don't.
It's fighting to believe herself

no matter what.
It's the fury she feels every time

she has to make herself compact
and the terrible,

immense tenderness
of being held

by the world,
then dropped.

She has been dreaming
of searchlights again.

They sweep slowly
and with purpose

over frozen fields.

YOU DO NOT HAVE TO BE
THE SAME FOREVER

NEW YORK IN JUNE

I'm not sure how I stayed alive
the summer I lost you.
I hardly noticed the sky,
refused to learn from it,
drew lines through your name.
I rode the train alone,
walked home alone,
worked every night
serving ice cream by the pier
to bury the risk and joy
and despair of you.
I drank rum in the back
with the other servers,
watched Manhattan brighten
through glass
as my shift ended.
I missed Pittsburgh,
snowfall, the smell
of pine and chlorine,
childhood,
days lacking
any kind of order.
I never asked god about you.
It was an experiment:
I dissolved into staircases,
stations, rose and descended
eternally. I felt
like a fortress,
punished but intact.
I couldn't blame the heat
for its brutal rise.
The fires felt right.
Weary beyond words,
I walked in circles,
petals stuck to the soles
of my sandals.
I memorized
the aftermath
and let you go.

NIGHT RUNNER

I'm never sure how to wash stars
from my hair, each follicle rinsed with those barbs,
headache after headache calling tendons
into motion. Night runner, I ran.

I juxtaposed ankle
to tar, fell and fractured the metatarsal bone.

So what, I fell, I stood up, kept walking,
ripped space from cuticle,
brain stem, crumbling infinitesimal
sparks into ash, ash, ash:

there is anguish in movement but I have to move,
go to work—what use are studies and predictions

to force, the flash in my muscles that says *here, now,*
who am I? That's who. I stood up. What can you mend
when you too dissolve into pixels, 1 gram
of imagistic fragments? What's left? 6-8 weeks,

elevate the foot, sit still and rest, while the earth is quaking?
Motion, anemia, osteoporosis, night runner unbeats

the heart into living. Where is calcium in space?
How will I know what remains if I stop,
and the ache ends? I will forget how you look.
Get me up. I was one ache away from understanding.

I couldn't move, didn't know what I was comprised of
until it had to be repaired.

YOU DO NOT HAVE TO BE CURED

PSYCHOANALYSIS

Your tired brain floats above you.
A nest of water forms against your tongue.

There are too many sunflowers
in your wrist muscles;

he can see them opening.
The psychological term for happiness

is *subjective wellbeing*, and he is worried
about yours. There are indications:

a rush of cortisol down a highway
of parasympathetic nerves, a whole

biological field of moods waiting to be defined.
How many diseases still have to be invented?

You have created a world in which you are the patient
and everything else is your personal psychologist

including the porch with roses, and all of the tomb-like
winters that bury it from view.

Even your silence starts talking as you lie down.
It points to the parts of it that hurt.

IN THE PINES

If I'm there, in that image,
I'm alive.

Even if it's dark,
I'm vibrant.

If you hear the owl sing,
don't go.

If you're not telling me anything,
who are you?

I turn over a pinecone
in my hand.

Something scratches,
imprints snow.

It might as well be you,
fraying the night.

Something lies
under the enormous pine.

The shadows in that space
tell their own truths.

If I'm evidence,
is this ruined?

If you say
fantasy, it can't sing.

If you act like everything
is normal, there's an official

cause of death.
I'm not even going to

name the people
in those photos
if you don't.

THE QUESTIONS WE ASK OF LIFE RETURN AS WOLVES

For more time with her I would cast
pieces of myself into orbit.

I bargain: take one year of my life
and let her stay in the world.

When she goes into remission,
I'm reckless, an engine ignited—

hard to tell if the universe obeyed,
but my lifeline looks the same,

extended by a scar
from an old knife wound.

Years ago, she pulled a blade
across my palm. I did not expect

the cut, my fascination
at the glimpse of fat and bone.

The ER doctor wanted to arrest her,
pulled synthetic sutures through flesh.

I did not flinch. The doctor said
I'd make a good ship captain,

as in, I'd leave the burning ship last.
As I mended, years and years

were added to my life,
as was this wolfish longing.

Uncertainty bothers her more.
I say: why shouldn't it?

YOU DO NOT HAVE TO KEEP TIME

INTO FOCUS

Throw your voice into this valley and it comes back
a mountain, she said, hers rising so unpredictably
I could barely keep sight of her. I called out, *Anyone!*

Anyone, anyone. I know how my voice sounds
in terms of the delphinium, the snakeskin,
the batwings, how little it means within the circuitry

of loss. We make room for the poems that crash
into windowpanes, or the poems that are slow
to come into focus. In calling out, I am calling
to myself. I don't know the conversation of existing

but I pick up fragments. It's useless
to examine our own skeletons. I have thrown
my bones into a starry grave, become the nothingness

of walking through a field of Queen Ann's Lace.
I would like to speak only with paper, everything else
overwhelming with its calling back and forth, its vanishing.

PLACE OF SHELTER

In Dublin, foxes circled the basilicas. The chorus of their estrangement
distorted the greenness of ground-swells. Their furs inflected dusk
as they roved the city's inner ear. In Italy, my sister had a fox tattooed

on her floating rib. Lean and red, drawn mid-leap, it healed itself
with paws raised, a sketch more delicate than honeycomb.

The foxes traced my path on nights I walked through Rathmines,
gliding into sight from the blackthorn hedges. Green bottles
between us, green glass and roadkill, our paws crushed blossoms

in the leftover streetlight. Apprehension of night's end. I prayed
to stall the sunrise. A fact that only vixens scream, polyphonic

sequences of separate warning. The males nudge the turf, upset
the rabbit dens. Restless, I scrutinized the warden's flashlight
and climbed the stone wall, past curfew, hunting seabirds, scuffed

my kneecap on ancient spikes of rusted iron. Home rowed
further away from me, penalty for drifting off on my magnetic voyage.

Had to guess at god, had to study the escarpments of another continent.
I could feel America replacing me. I found in these nocturnal animals
tenderhearted priests, regal in their photospheric howls.

As long as steeples held the firmament, we could sprint away
before dawn, when protestors rallied to fight abortion laws.

We could save our garnet, our blood-red, our pollen. We could
flee the shaming banners where the holy surf was calm.

MEDICINAL PROPERTIES

Instructions for healing
are written inside my own silent cells,
or buried within your voice as you read
the final lines of a story and forget
I am lying beside you.

I don't want muscle and shape,
or the distractions of size, or change's
spectacular ramifications. I want stability
against a final loss of everything entangled,
glittering away insignificantly
a leaf appearing and falling
from an invisible branch.

I think it is my memory of being shaped
that wants the imagined nothingness
they say is lodged so deeply in the truth;
it shoots down my arms as I eat, sleep,
shake, run, sit, brief traveling waves.

Of course it is crucial to want a bandage
torn from someone else's clothes, to wish
relentlessly for the consistency of definition
between one place and another.

REMEMBERING WHAT THE BODY IS

You are speaking with your fingertips into an aperture,
lean arms burnt, ventricles wired to flowering strings
of shaved-down air and flattening sparks: this is the bed
at eight a.m., nine a.m., your body remembering what
the body is, a torn-up experiment, anatomical fragments.

Vomit afterwards because the mouth must open darkly.
With hospital curtain drawn, I record your intake.
It must be a pill, a precisely yellow pill, a ghost-swallowed pill,
a pill of acid rain to crush and drink before bed, a fluorescent pill,
five hundred pills suspended in the esophagus, iron and ink,

crushed along the jaw becoming wax, a terrain, a tundra,
an artful and elegant pill, a chord of pills in a tiny cup,
your brain smothered in antiseptic pills, take five,
five hundred, take without food, without help, without
burnt white tea vitamin water, a very unfeeling

and blood-stained pill. You're safer and closer,
you're safe, there is nothing but corridors of pills
and gowns sewed up with pills and water and waiting
for a cloud to assemble, nothing but taking a pill that blooms
and embalms, floods the tongue with weight.

YOU DO NOT HAVE TO BE MIGHTY

DECONSTRUCTION

Watching a stranger carry your broken bed
down three flights of stairs

reminds me of linen wrapped around a hand
and I don't know where you are

and perhaps I am still thoroughly asleep
and thriving on the dreams of you

that dart around me.
I wonder where you live now

and if anything has changed,
anything: an anchor growing still

saying everything's gone: not
as long as I'm wrapped in simple

cloth, careful with how I love,
careful: the stranger props one half of the bed

against a date palm. Its copper leaves
are awake with your voice. The bed's

second half is still stuck inside,
hinges and clamor, small scraps of song.

I think of you here, shaking his hand.
I think of the nest we saw built into brick.

VOLTA

How did I find your door in the dark? I mean dark
like the hand cupped around the hipbone.
I mean darker than hallways of obsolete places,

a friend's new apartment darker than what we did,
unzipping love's black dress so it became a pool,

a hole in the floor, then climbing the black ladder down
to fix it all. It was an ecstatic search as always
a search of infinitely retraced, re-learned actions.

I buckled my boots, rolled my heart in firedust,
Walt Whitman's sunset bleeding through the folds

of someone else's map. My map was soaked through
by the time I found you, told you I tried to kick love,
pull love from the spine of midnight.

We made no mention of what we were doing,
transcending the borders, consoling each other

as the barriers fell. We made no excuses, entered
the vacuum of listening, caring for one another
our voices replaced by the vocabulary of all

that quickly closes. You turned the lights down,
took my eyes away. It was more than I am usually

capable of, falling fast through the earth
walking straight into the dark
believing it will not follow.

SIDE EFFECTS

You're caught in this loophole, a story with no pictures.

(It begins with a shock table, head braced, counting
        down.)

Electrodes stuck firmly to the forehead. *Ten, nine.*

Bi-lateral, targeting both sides of the brain, convulsions
        softened

with sedatives, what's the word? *Four, three.*

Picture a flamethrower shot into a cavern, eye sockets
        igniting.

Memory, see also: flinching

in chemicals. Infantile stillness, jaw relaxed,
        the nervous system

trying to reset. Do you know what day it is? *Clear.*

Picture this, a spider breathing, mute tremendous breath.
        Can you respond?

Most patients don't remember seizing. In fact,

nothing you remember is possible. Feather
        in a coma,

teeth buzzing. Blank unwired screen, what's your

mood, 1-10? Last resort, it takes one shock,
        you fold the dark.

YOU DO NOT HAVE TO GENERATE
CAPITAL

SOME ANSWERS I WROTE ON A LONG TERM DISABILITY QUESTIONNAIRE

Are your illnesses, injuries, or conditions related to your work in any way?

I got caught up in the destructive gravity of Sagittarius A* and paid the price.

Are you still unable to work because of your illnesses, injuries, or conditions?

If an object is moving toward us, its spectral lines shift to shorter wavelengths;
if it's moving away the lines swing to longer wavelengths.
The higher velocity, the greater the shift.

Have you filed, or do you intend to file, for any other public disability benefits?

This could happen if the ejected stars came from a stellar disk
surrounding the supermassive black hole.

When do you believe your condition(s) became severe enough
to keep you from working (even if you have never worked)?

We do not have a complete survey of the entire sky. However,
theorists believe that the Milky Way is surrounded by a triaxial
[football-shaped] distribution of dark matter.

You may use this space for any explanation. If you need more space,
attach a separate sheet. If unknown, check "unknown."

How much the trajectories deviate, and in what direction they do this,
depend on the shape and orientation of the dark matter halo.

I have been here so many times before.

TRANSCRANIAL MAGNETIC STIMULATION

Surgical marker
runs along my hairline
and turns my shampoo purple.

I lose days to a hospital wing
disguised as a quiet
apartment complex.

While I do nothing
with this year, my sisters
return to school;

they take Advanced Italian,
Art History, Human Memory,
Art Theft, Statistics,

Studio Art: Printmaking
or they begin to sing
sweeter versions

of themselves, while here—
Nothing, the technician says.
Nothing again.

I'm awake to hear him
and to see my hand
motionless beside me,

a paper flower
refusing to tremble.
It defends itself against

the bright room,
a white cube,
death—it won't *forget.*

The coil
moves over
my skull

in search of
a motor threshold.
Resistance is unusual, he says,

but it happens to some.
(Nothing)
It might be painful

if we continue.
I've been watching
the year through

different lenses,
x-rays, shutters
closing over each month.

A private knowledge forms:
who I was then
was so unprepared

for who I am now.
Some people ask:
What will you do after?

If after arrives,
I'll be grateful
to medicine

for making
gardens out of the
long silences

in my brain.
Grateful for
the failure of

encoding,
storage,
and retrieval.

Some things

shouldn't be
remembered.

YOUR OWN PERSONAL ESCAPE CHUTE

Sweetheart, the battlefield is ringing with alarm bells
and they call that *presence*, the *stratosphere*, your only
opposition the tranquilizer gun you aim at yourself when
you need sleep, your blood looks like flint glass, horsetail,
but we need you to save yourself first even though
it's hard not to abandon people's imitations of empathy,
RIP, and prisoners who got away from the loophole
of chaos scrambling time. The hospital is no place
for the indifferent. I don't joke about what kills
the literally haunted satellite humming through us
but try to outsprint the hazy, the unaware, the lesions
in focus, it all fits together, the drama of "let me
comfort you," try to zero in on the somewhere patch of grass
that is as outdated as the bullets coming, do not be paralyzed
by the pH balances permanently set or whatever else
lengthens the moment. Sit yourself down in this inside-out
instruction. Thumbs up, love. What else is there to say?

LONG TERM DISABILITY FORM ANSWERS, CONTINUED

Place of birth:

> I was always outspoken.

Speak English:

> YES

Read English:

> YES

Currently married:

> There's a lifetime of emotions
> or a sense of bewilderment,
> something truthful about all of us,
> a tragic sense of existence.

Have any children:

> (You still need a telescope
> to resolve them from each other.)

Any other names used:

> We communicate in many ways.
> Our galaxy is in constant transition,
> overexposed in this image.

Any prior marriages:

> Stars in our neighborhood
> have a lot of empty space between them;
> they will not collide.

Diagnosed with a condition expected to end in death?

> Yes.
> But that's not the astonishing part.

YOU DO NOT HAVE TO BE INNOCENT

FORMS OF SUSPENSION

The body is safe in the mirror. The mirror is not in control
of every sacrifice. Two lovers kneel between two mirrors.
They are trading bones. They mean for you to see it.

Between two mirrors the lovers break open, gathering each other
and wanting privacy. The mirrors hold the lovers in place,
recording their thousand inseparable positions.

DON'T YOU

A note is off, but I can't tell which, and I've fucked up,
but we're on the same page. *Do you love me?*
you don't remember asking. Yes I do, your shirts
smell good, and I like when you talk about biology,
saying the body does this, does that, show me. You slip
your note cards into my dress, they fall out one by one,
we're dancing and then we're walking to the diner
and you have quarters for a song,
you choose the longest one of all, the worst,
maybe I've learned all I need to know
and our friends black out on the apartment floor,
we draw constellations between their shoes,
their party clothes, we scratch their elbows
with a fine-tip pen, and no one knows the name
of the person sleeping in the corner, he's holding
my pillow and looking at peace with some greater part
of the universe, *that kid's gone,* you say, and
he is, he is. Tomorrow I'll untangle my body from yours,
face the daylight spread across the wall.
It's happening now and happens all the time,
and I'll be awake before you and our friends
making sure all of them are breathing, collecting
pieces of myself from them, from you.

THE HEART SHUTS

My father says grief is a kind of wrath, a building of armor.
Grief is a kind of death.
I want to know, will a gold shield save us?

—

After a parent dies, a student writes to say
that though her heart has not stopped from grief,
she will be absent.

She writes: *It's my fault.*
The words dim and glitter like dew on the screen: *my fault.*
They glow like a lunar x-ray.

Dear one, I want to write, *it's not.*
But this compassion does not look
or sound professional.

—

My father thinks death is the dark backing we need
for the mirror to work, the mirror in which
we see ourselves and all our calibrations.

When my heart went dull, he was there
with a deck of cards
and lilies at the hospital.

At the intake I was asked: Are your parents
proud of you? I could hear the ticking clock,
the faceless forms.

—

My father loves Westerns and when I ask him why
he shrugs. He likes the Wild West, the music,
thunder and rain, horses and shootouts,

and when a cowboy says:

Alive or dead it's your choice
I get it.

—

We watch his mother die together.
We are onlookers, immobile,
and there's no stopping it.

Later we break down laughing
at how, days before, when the doctor asked
what he could do to help,

my grandmother said,
Yeah, find a cure for cancer.
Crying, he says, *Damn.*

—

He carried me from the car
to the emergency room
and my head was full of asters,

the migraine setting in,
blue fingertips,
nothing much to say.

The hardest thing:
to ask nothing of life
when you are roped to it.

—

Grief made me an object, a facet, an ambulance
I didn't ask for, and my friends sent letters
that I strung above my bed like darts to throw

at the moving paper target of recovery.
I had to say goodbye to absolutes—
my dying wouldn't bring anyone back—

no spells, no countermagic, could.
Defenseless, grief is a fired gun,
a showdown, a geranium; it's a form of order,

a relapse, an echo that travels
from screen to screen, star to star
while you stand at the center with the horses.

VALOR

My father and his cousins used to roam
Tinley Park all night while their fathers,
steelworkers, fought it out in a basement
on Minnesota Avenue. The fights weren't
just about money—they were about
owning the time-worn rules of fighting
through swift blows to the head and gut,
and my father knew good form:
stand sideways, make yourself flicker
like the sound of breaking glass, burn hotter
than venom spat up with silver teeth and blood.
Punch with your whole body. In dreams
I walk with him: picture construction sites
and loose change, push-ups, cigarettes,
and indestructible will. I was born first,
oldest daughter steeled for conflict,
and he prepared me for a world
that would take, made me rise, ice-ribbed,
nimble. I learned how to make a fist,
how to spot a liar, how to look a thief
in the eye. Now, side by side,
we stitch and unstitch the violence
we inherited, talking of ruin
and survival, honor and fidelity,
mending and refitting our cracked armor,
begging my sisters to be kinder.

YOU DO NOT HAVE TO KNOW

RETELLING

There was one who did not return—
the boy in my high school who inhaled gauze

before the anesthesiologist could bring him back
to the same room where they took out

four of my teeth, cotton rolled against my gums.
There must be room for error in every procedure

but I want to know if he heard, lying down,
the light spray of water in his mouth,

or the summer heat that makes it hard to inhale,
heat that stays wrapped up in the lungs.

My sisters give me a lucky pomegranate seed
as if they know how close we are to going under.

Some say luck itself is simple, but have you ever
felt luck unlock wrong, held your hand

against the wall that luck broke down
so you could fix wrong and live with certain losses,

so you could match the groove in every brick
that pinned you to the ground,

luck nothing more but a tongue that moves.

TRYING TO SWIM

A song lyric makes its slow way, sings
behind rules and steps and fumes,

a sound beyond language strung in the water,
the might of the sea

around my shoulders—
I still don't know how I got here,

the Pacific transported, transposed,
and the urgent mind sirens, signals,

turning my arms in circles.
I remember doing this with my mother,

gliding in waves and wading
toward crash and tow

back when losing her
seemed impossible—

and there are other moments,
but they are nowhere fluttering in cold salt,

and I did not allow myself to dive as far before,
she was always watching, refused

to leave a swimmer unobserved—
and there is nothing that ceases to be,

it's just this, there is only this *now*
without her, the fracturing of sound that belongs

to another realm, a tide
whose source is verse and song.

YOU DO NOT HAVE TO CREATE PARADISE

DREAMSCAPE WITH EMBRYO

In my dream you were grape-sized
and wanted milk.

I had sparkling water, no milkbottle,
but I watched you bloom,

you who I might never give birth to
because of my life is governed

by medicine.
Is there a remedy?

Last winter I sat in the library
as though inside the beak of a bird

reading a study on women who stopped
their medications in order to become pregnant.

Many terminated one third of the way through,
as life had become dire, unlivable.

I pressed the pages flat
with fingertips like kerosene.

Child who my father so badly wants to meet,
should I pass on this lineage of pills,

the mirrors, curved spines, and anxiety,
the postpartum and hospital gowns—to you?

Would you be like me, undoing
the latticework of your body

with rituals when pain splinters
the nesting bowl? I would

talk you through it. Once,
I told my mother that being alive

meant always being worried
about death. I would rather

be a drop in the ocean,
prismatic.

Ungrateful!
If you weren't born, how could you

be loved? she said.
Must something

be conscious
in order to be loved?

Little fleck of gold,
tell me what you want.

I'll clear the area,
dilate, iron-infused,

see what I can make
with blood and flesh,

wait at the ruby-red
station of withdrawal

to stop shaking,
for sleep to return.

I know the risks:
uncontrollable crying,

seizures, delirium,
vomiting, tremors.

Soft anonymous:
let me know.

You do not have to
be grateful.

YOU DO NOT HAVE TO BE GOOD

When you move away you see how much time depends
on the people you love—how much relies on the second
your father returns home and hands you his suit coat
while the papers in his briefcase settle and you must
recite an event from the day. Time relies on his exit

from the kitchen. Time depends on the existence of the living room
where he plays Greensleeves on the guitar you almost ruined.
It makes me cry to understand him through the songs
he taught himself. Time relies on the Casio whose tiny keys
we pressed together. I guess he is my first real memory of sound.

I sat in the guitar case while he re-strung. He never asked
what I was going to make of my life. He expected
that it would be exceptional, although he often faulted me
for wandering away, for filling the neighbor's mailbox
with water balloons, but I was raised by a man who set off

cherry bombs in his neighbors' yards. Time relies
on the moment he was abandoned by his parents
in South Bend, Chicago. His mother occasionally
left groceries on the porch. Last summer I saw him
pacing the living room, hands in his pockets,

he was listening to football. He finally looked relaxed.
It was exhausting to have three girls, a triumvirate of drama
but so much sincerity of feeling, we wrecked the house
with our instruments and clothes, we overturned the calm
with saxophones, flutes, cymbals, trumpets, drum machines

and talent show rehearsals. We gave him the tiny spoons
at dinner, we left streaks of nailpolish on his legal papers,
we picked the lock on his briefcase and hid his car keys,
left notes. Have a good day! I love you so much. Every note
he ever left me, I kept. Have a nice day, he wrote. Be good.

AND NOW THERE IS NO MORE BLUE

as though a certain fruit split open
and stained the air in a way I am not
imagining, as though the surface of his
turquoise ring changed to gray
in a way nothing should change
when touched, as though the surface
of the lake turned dark green when
the swans left—dramatic, as it must be,
the ritual of giving up blue, the sudden decision
not to see it, his decision to come to me broken
like they all do, because he wants me to perform
a different ritual with what light's left.
Where are we? What else is in the room?
It still matters. He touches my ear
searching for the stray, unattainable—
wanting to catch hold of it. He leans
into me, which is what the sea can do
and it's the same people, same music,
same ghosts I couldn't forget from the very
start. I promised not to use less force
and by this, I meant several things:
I'd do what not everyone does,
I'd become arctic like the edges
of his body, and I wouldn't give in
to loss and more loss even when
he indicated that it was enough.
Still: I look at him now through no particular body,
moved just enough to think I've found it...
the green that means something, an arrow,
a hunger is being ripped out of me
and there is a kind of music to it
that I don't regret, or pity, and why
shouldn't it matter, I try to say to him,
that it was so rough, that what
bruised me bruised you.

CLOCKWORK

His daydreams are about death, his father,
and sex. I know his gentleness is often
overlooked, but the way he sees—
camera facedown on the table
lifted, aimed—is the way I see.
Gentleness, death, books
unread, art unseen, living hungry
for art, for love, like clockwork
the schedule, the structure, is internal
and the trains come or they don't
and we die or we don't. In the museum,
the world's oldest piano is surrounded
by visitors. Darkness translates into
magnificent gold, Byzantine coins in a row.
I'm talking to the marble face in the vitrine
as if her body has been recovered.
I'm backing away from the wall of negatives
the artist will develop, or won't.
The thrown-out art is on display.
It means more to me than it should
that when you approach me,
the images arise, chemical, intaglio,
permanent, all too inexpressible
and you are the only one who sees them.
At eight, at ten, at midnight, a memory
breaks up traffic. I remember your
boxes of instruments filled with hundreds
of extinguished signals. To contradict
a death, one must believe they can
still hear a sunrise. I try to repeat this
plainly and without alarm,
a sound descended from the lyre.

YOU DO NOT HAVE TO MEASURE THE LONGITUTE AND LATITUDE

MY COUSIN THE ASTRONAUT

My cousin Andrew (Drew) Morgan made his first flight into
outer space aboard the Soyuz MS-13 spacecraft headed for
the International Space Station in July 2019.

He departed from the Baikonur Cosmodrome in Kazakh-
stan (12:28 p.m. EST launch). He will be in space for nine
months. For more information visit NASA.gov.

Can he see the wall, the cathedrals,
sanctuaries, raids, cages holding bodies captive,
mothers torn from children?

Is his view obscured by clouds of dust?

On earth, we wait for papers to arrive;
they never do.

We receive warnings on bright yellow stationery:

This notice does not grant any immigration status or benefit.

Have we ever:

Engaged in any unlawful commercialized vice?
Practiced polygamy?

Within the past ten years,
been a prostitute or procured
anyone for prostitution?

We sign our names for electronic capture.

—

Dear government, we have some questions.
For example, is the president a hologram? Tell us:

What ignites supernova explosions?
How can we spot satellite triads?

What's life like at the remotest telescopes?
What's the density of a black hole?

—

USCIS will schedule a specific date, time, and place
where you will have your fingerprints and photographs taken.

See the appointment notice. If you want to reschedule,
you must do so in writing.

—

Earth and space
are alive with transmissions.

I want to know why
there is no consistent theory

about the state of matter
within a black hole,

whatever "within"
means.

What I really want to know:
in space, do politics dissolve?

Does infinity exist?

Nothing / nobody—
how does it feel?

What is the sun worth?

Does night,
electric, endless,
solve any problems?

Do our conflicts
become any less important
at a distance?

—

My student studies space law.
His classmates tease him:

Isn't space the only place with no rules?
But there are laws as firm

as constellations: they address debris,
interference, launch procedures, damage

to the surface of the earth, shielding,
ownership, control, what to do with pieces

that cannot be "tracked"
with any certainty, derelict satellites,

trash removal. There are rules.
In some ways, space is earth-like:

actions are punishable.
You could disappear forever.

—

A child contemplates infinity for the first time:

Does the universe have edges? If so, where?
What surrounds the universe? Where does it end?

He is taught that heaven is skyward—

wounds, saints, souls, where do they go?
He is told that sin will take him underground,

far below the earth's surface. He must confess

every wrongdoing. He is told that men
who love men

will spend the afterlife burning.

The moon is a communion tablet
that minds its own business

while his questions open wide
to swallow him whole.

—

How does it feel to see the world small?

Is the material that falls into a black hole
destroyed, or re-emitted?

Stars, silversmiths—I have questions.
I don't speak with angels, but I know

my capacity for love
encompasses all genders.

Visibility:
some say it doesn't matter.

I say: to know and be known
is an astronomical event.

—

Dear cousin, from a distance,
would you call earth

paradise? Is there a unity
to it all?

—

My parents sit watching
a broadcast of my cousin
entering the International Space Station.

When he climbs through the hatch,
we scream his name. He cries,
hanging in the void, happy

in the paper-thin air.
There is a woman
beside him.

Her hair floats
around her shoulders
in amber spirals.

The hatch they crawl through
swirls behind them
like a fingerprint.

ESCALATION

The guide asks us to follow him up the muddy hill
through furious rain. My boots slide and catch the roots

of fir trees whose crowns are hidden by white fog.
We climb the sloped path up the side of the mountain's

soil and moss. These gentle attachments remind me
of who is no longer here anymore. I wish you were.

In lightheaded increments we ascend. My sisters
trail behind with water. The footpath is steep,

overlooks turquoise and sulfuric yellow hot springs.
The national park was halfway burned down by wildfires.

Black bears settle in the fog and when we scare them
it's because the woods themselves are troubled.

I lighten my steps and fear my obvious heat.
You were someone whose transformations

I found hard to understand. How evaporative,
to confront this hemisphere. I try not to think

that I am also dying, but the brassy leaves confuse me.
Flare and burn yellow where you are, look back.

We move on, climb toward the summit's boulders.

SAY IT

What do you want,
child mad enough
to try? You couldn't

be smaller.
Malnourished hand
in the moon,

scarred and flowering:
proof you can hear,
you can see.

Break the pact
with your body.
You are not that armor.

Break it off,
that fusion
no longer painful.

The body waits,
calling you back
when you're ready.

You've done nothing
unforgivable. Say it.
Transform many times.

Change is your flint,
use it to renew. Say it:
you want to live.

I DREAM OF YOU FURIOUSLY

What does the painter see inside your face,
cheekbone hollowing slowly as you turn, a drape
of black hair hanging at the back of your dress
covering a calm symmetry turned loose?
What stillness makes him want to paint you?

I see now what he can never un-see, and wish
I could snap his brushes away, use his chemical
soap to scrub off charcoal clouds that glide
around his hands as if parting your hair's
cutting waves; I see your glasslike imbalances
and self-cancellations, your shoulder blades
rendering a perfect midpoint that looks

so surprising and intensely calm as you lift
your hand in a landscape of topiary, safe at first
but concealing something terrible, a sensuous
celebration of black nail polish worse than ever before.
I see love that flesh brings us before it becomes
ragged like arrows passing their targets, exiting

the human eye, exceedingly opulent and lost
like most things we are made of. I feel pulled
by the growing tug of commitment as something
in you splits noticeably, glacial affectionate
hailstones falling with elegant undercutting sweeps
throwing what he is making into the endless sea
of your body's impossible blessings.

YOU DO NOT HAVE TO BE RIGOROUS

MAGICAL ACTS

Present me with the greater half
of your sacrifice.

May I look at your hands?
May I press your hands

into my temples, may I pick apples
cracked by the sun, may I become

saint-like, resurrect memories,
and if I am incapable of memory,

may I speak with my mother?
The figure of my father says no

and makes corrections
when I turn my back.

The embassy of food has collapsed
over this little conference of wounds.

Someone will grab me by the throat
if they're unhappy.

I think I'll let the pressure
become great enough

to launch a spacecraft into
the blood-red mood of the evening.

When my father advises me
on goodness,

his eyes are off somewhere
in the fieldless end

as he decides how he should
deal with me. My problem is motion,

limbs held beneath unbroken ice.
I have never been this close

to the fissure between restraint
and restraint's materials.

He will also one day soften
but for now he makes a speech,

my father, calling hunger all across
America. I protest, courteous but shaken,

isolated, intractable. I'm waiting
for the arc in his voice to run out

and behind my face make a fire;
restraint becomes the only

grave in my nightmare.
Hunger the only regime.

DIAGNOSIS

I do not call you out of your hideaway.
No one knows how much time. I do not say,
How much time? I do not make offerings.
I do not shake out the wreath of hearts
that circles me, drumming like something
immense is near. I do not make way for the cold.
I burn it out, setting every room to this furnace,
skylights blazing. I understand that answers
come in different forms, and on their own time,
sweeping out the dark with little warning.
This morning eight babies strapped into two large strollers
passed me at the crosswalk. They were flushed
with wind, cropped hair askew. I did not ask for
a time table, or a pile of sand. I did not feel marked
by a vanishing point. I thought their faces
looked clairvoyant, conscious of a process that
at most times I am not. I did not stare
long enough to see it.

DISTRACTION

I hope you live an extraordinary life,
a long and passionate hundred years,
small girl with a leaf in your hand.
I was you, watching the rain intently,
digging for seeds in a field of pumpkins,
spitting at the tires of passing bicycles.
You bring a seashell to your father's bed
set it on his hand, and drift from there.
The sheet covering his thin legs
rises and falls sharply at his knees.
He keeps a bottle of pills on the table.
Nurses keep entering the room,
taking him through the standard procedures.
My job is to keep you occupied
while they make the incisions,
to keep you unsuspecting as they fly
his body between hospitals. I draw
a triangle with chalk for you to stand inside,
put ten raspberries on your fingertips
while you laugh hysterically.
Someone's love will keep you going.
I don't know whose. I know you are too small
to ever fall out of my sight.

YOU DO NOT HAVE TO PROVE IT

I SEE HER AMONG THE STARS

Mary looked through the telescope
at Betelgeuse, the brightest star in Orion
and one of the largest known stars;
it marks the western shoulder
of the constellation.
She wanted to know,
will it explode?
And God said, yes it will.
The star Betelgeuse will run out of fuel,
collapse under its own weight
and then rebound in a supernova explosion.
When?
And God said, probably not soon.
It was January. She felt
like a feather in a teacup
haloed in gold foil.
She learned the star chart
by mid-May, glimpsed
Orion briefly in the west
and had to ask:
So we're safe from Betelgeuse?
Well, He said, if there are any astronomers
around when it does blow, they will be extremely
thrilled to have a nearby supernova.
She nodded. Said:
Even if it's nearing the end of its life,
I do love the golden colors
of Betelgeuse against
a velvetly black night sky.
So turn, He said, and live.

FLOOD THE VOID

Tell me I am good despite everything.
Sing me one of your songs
as you carry me upstairs.
Tell me all the friends I don't see anymore
made, and make, me happy.
Find me a field of broken irises.

A boy runs down the street
with silver balloons tied to his wrist.
I can hear the flood of color.
I'd like to think you're the kind of person
who comes from a dysfunctional home
but never uses the word *broken*.

And you might be able to detect
the details of the forest's shimmering edge
in my brain, faint green-gold
that intensifies at night,
heavenly trees on the periphery,
bark on fire for someone.

Do you have an ice tray?
Tell me that I will feel terrible if I steal
a string of lights from a stranger's lawn.
Throw me over your shoulder
when I don't believe you, piercing
glow on the back of my hands.

Will you cook something for me?
Do you freeze blueberries,
line up your shoes for the afterlife?
Do you have a shirt I can borrow?
Have we gone beyond the periphery
with a mind to get through it?

Carry me through the cemetery
over unsteady ground.
Kiss me among the graves.
Tell me I have several lives
and this is the truest one.

Acknowledgments

Many thanks to the editors and staff of the following publications in which versions of these poems first appeared:

Fields Magazine: "THE BLUE OF IT"

Jai-Alai Magazine: "PLACE OF SHELTER"

The Literary Nest: "DECONSTRUCTION" and "DIG"

Oakland Review Alumni Edition: "SLEEP PHASE" and "FLOOD THE VOID"

Oakland Review: "REMEMBERING WHAT THE BODY IS"

PANK Magazine: "SURROUND HER WITH COLORS"

Pleiades: "SMALLNESS"

Pittsburgh Poetry Review: "FORTY BLACK SHIPS" and "VULNERARY"

Plain China: "INTO FOCUS"

Poetry Leaves Anthology: "I SEE HER AMONG THE STARS"

Prelude: "TO CHARGE FORWARD"

riverSedge: "A DREAM IN MOTION"

The Scores: "NIGHT WORK"

Show Us Your Papers Anthology–Main Street Rag: Version of "FOLLOWING MY PARENTS WITH A CAMERA"

Three Rivers Review: "CHILD MAD ENOUGH," "NIGHT RUNNER," "SIDE EFFECTS"

Voices from the Attic, Edited by Jan Beatty: "DON'T YOU"

Yew Journal: "INSIDE THE METROPOLIS"

A selection of poems were published in the chapbook, *The Mark My Body Draws in Light*: Finishing Line Press (2014).

Loving Thanks

To Bryn Dodson, for everything.

To Deborah Landau, my New York University MFA thesis advisor and mentor, for believing in my work. To Jim Daniels of Carnegie Mellon University for supporting my poetry endeavors for over a decade. To Catherine Barnett, whose luminous chaos and order poetry workshop shaped this manuscript and taught me how to teach. To my sisters Julia and Emma, and my siblings-in-law, Molly, Hayley, and Kris. To my parents, Robert Barnes and Michelle Maher, for the gifts of life and poetry. To my family in Australia, especially Kris and Allen Dodson, for love that spans continents. To relatives alive and dead whose unconditional love is deeply felt.

To the following workshops, institutions, and organizations: the Madwomen In the Attic (you have my heart always), The New York State Summer Writers Institute, the Chautauqua Writer's Center, the Vermont Studio Center, the Center for Book Arts, the Poetry Ireland Introductions, the John Woods Scholarship, Carnegie Mellon University's English Department and College of Fine Arts, Trinity College Dublin, and The Graduate Center, CUNY.

To my dear friends who have read endless versions of this manuscript, especially Sebastian Doherty, Emma Hine, Linda Harris Dolan, Anna Meister, Raquel Dorman, and Neil Aitken—thank you for your insight and encouragement. To the Lunar Walk Poetry Series crew, especially Gerry LaFemina and Lynn McGee. To North Allegheny teachers and staff, especially Antonio Caruso, Cyd Stackhouse, Diane Feliciani, Lance Rhinehart, Carol Psych, Joe Harvey, Karen Goodman, Robert Bricker, and Jody Williams. To Dan Toski, Melissa Dias-Mandoly, Carrie Wellbaum, Anna Israel, and Edye Pucciarelli. To Julie Mallis and Hannah Rule and our Treehouse in Pittsburgh. To my collaborators, including Jiyoo Jye. To my brilliant cohort, classmates, colleagues, and friends from over the years who continue to push ahead with their own radiant creative work—there are more of you than I can name and I love you all. To my students, whose humor and creativity make everything worthwhile, and to my beloved teachers and workshop leaders, especially Ellen McGrath Smith, Joy Katz, Sharon Olds, Wayne Koestenbaum, Jan Beatty, Anne Carson, and Terrance Hayes. To the

Many Louise Glücks. To Joel W. Coggins for this incredible book cover and years of friendship. To Chris Lucas and Matt Wofsy. To Cate Clother and our fierce Cordella community.

To my poetic and artistic heroes and muses: Rainer Maria Rilke, Carolyn Forché, bell hooks, Galway Kinnell, Federico García Lorca, Sylvia Plath, James Baldwin, Adrienne Rich, Sappho, Louise Glück, Frida Kahlo, Paul Cézanne, Patti Smith, Virginia Woolf, and especially Mary Oliver, with whom this manuscript is in conversation.

To Matt Mauch, Tayve Neese, and Sara Lefsyk—thank you for championing this book and giving it a fighting chance. Thank you for your many inspired edits, patience, support, and the brilliant labor of love that is Trio House Press.

I wrote this book especially for queer disabled women and non-binary folks, and for girls and non-binary teens whose creativity was taken advantage of by men in positions of power in the literary community. To those who remain invisible and suffer silently due to stigma and ableism, to the rebels and misfits—this is for you.

About the Author

Madeleine Barnes is a poet, visual artist, and Doctoral Fellow in English Literature at the Graduate Center, CUNY. She is the author of three chapbooks: *Women's Work*, forthcoming from Tolsun Books, *Light Experiments* (Porkbelly Press, 2019), and *The Mark My Body Draws in Light* (Finishing Line Press, 2014). She serves as Poetry Editor at *Cordella Magazine*, a publication that showcases the work of women and non-binary creators. Named an emerging writer by the Poetry Ireland Introductions, she is the recipient of a John Woods Scholarship to study poetry in the Czech Republic, a New York Summer Writers Institute Fellowship, two Academy of American Poets poetry prizes, the Princeton Poetry Prize, the Gertrude Gordon Journalism Prize, and the Three Rivers Review Poetry Prize. She has exhibited artwork at The Miller Gallery (Pittsburgh, PA), Groundfloor Gallery (Brooklyn, NY), and Community Arts Phoenixville (Philadelphia, PA) and other galleries. She holds an MFA from New York University and an MPhil from Trinity College Dublin, and has taught creative writing, literature, and humanities research at New York University and Brooklyn College.

About the Book

You Do Not Have to Be Good was designed at Trio House Press through the collaboration of:

Matt Mauch, Lead Editor
Sara Lefsyk, Supporting Editor
Joel Coggins, Cover Design
Matt Mauch, Interior Design

The text is set in Adobe Caslon Pro.

The publication of this book is made possible, whole or in part,
by the generous support of the following individuals or agencies:

Anonymous

About the Press

Trio House Press is an independent literary press publishing three or more collections of poems annually. Our Mission is to promote poetry as a literary art enhancing culture and the human experience. We offer two annual poetry awards: the Trio Award for First of Second Book for emerging poets and the Louise Bogan Award for Artistic Merit and Excellence for a book of poems contributing in an innovative and distinct way to poetry. We also offer an annual open reading period for manuscript publication

Trio House Press adheres to and supports all ethical standards and guidelines outlined by the CLMP.

Trio House Press, Inc. is dedicated to the promotion of poetry as literary art, which enhances the human experience and its culture. We contribute in an innovative and distinct way to poery by publishing emerging and established poets, providing educational materials, and fostering the artistic process of writing poetry. For further information, or to consider making a donation to Trio House Press, please visit us online at www.triohousepress.org.

Other Trio House Press books you might enjoy:

X-Rays and Other Landscapes by Kyle McCord / 2019

Threed, This Road Not Damascus by Tamara J. Madison / 2019

My Afmerica by Artress Bethany White / 2018 Trio Award Winner selected by Sun Yung Shin

Waiting for the Wreck to Burn by Michele Battiste / 2018 Louise Bogan Award Winner selected by Jeff Friedman

Cleave by Pamel Johnson Parker / 2018 Trio Award Winner selected by Jennifer Barber

Two Towns Over by Darren C. Demaree / 2018 Louise Bogan Award Winner selected by Campbell McGrath

Bird~Brain by Matt Mauch / 2017

Dark Tussock Moth by Mary Cisper / 2016 Trio Award Winner selcted by Bhisham Bherwani

The Short Drive Home by Joe Osterhaus / 2016 Louise Bogan Award Winner selected by Chard DeNiord

Break the Habit by Tara Betts / 2016

Bone Music by Stephen Cramer / 2015 Louise Bogan Award Winner selected by Kimiko Hahn

Rigging a Chevy into a Time Machine and Other Ways to Escape a Plague by Carolyn Hembree / 2015 Trio Award Winner selected by Neil Shepard

Magpies in the Valley of Oleanders by Kyle McCord / 2015

Your Immaculate Heart by Annmarie O'Connell / 2015

The Alchemy of My Mortal Form by Sandy Longhorn / 2014 Louise Bogan Award Winner selected by Peter Campion

What the Night Numbered by Bradford Tice / 2014 Trio Award Winner selected by Carol Frost

Flight of August by Lawrence Eby / 2013 Louise Bogan Award Winner selected by Joan Houlihan

The Consolations by John W. Evans / 2013 Trio Award Winner selected by Mihaela Moscaliuc

Fellow Odd Fellow by Stephen Riel / 2013

Clay by David Groff / 2012 Louise Bogan Award Winner selected by Michael Waters

Gold Passage by Iris Jamahl Dunkle / 2012 Trio Award Winner selected by Ross Gay

If You're Lucky Is a Theory of Mine by Matt Mauch / 2012

CPSIA information can be obtained
at www.ICGtesting.com
Printed in the USA
BVHW031119280820
587381BV00003B/238